Digital Detox: 10 Easy Tips to Unplug and Recharge

By Zoel

WELCOME TO "DIGITAL DETOX: 10 EASY TIPS TO UNPLUG AND RECHARGE

In my personal life, I encountered the challenges of using technology and depending on it. It took me some time to realize that I was completely overwhelmed with the constant barrage of notifications demanding my immediate attention. I found myself caught in a cycle where my time was no longer my own, and I was pressured to be on my phone all day. Eventually, I burned out.

This book was born out of that experience. I realized I had to take back control of my time and not let technology dictate my life. I understood that under no circumstances should I give in to the pressures of being constantly connected. I saw how this digital catastrophe is affecting millions of people, and what's worse, our children are being targeted to spend endless hours on their phones. But there is hope. It is possible to save yourself and give yourself the time to detox from the digital world. This book is designed to guide you through practical and easy-to-follow steps to unplug and recharge. By implementing these tips, you can reclaim your time, reduce stress, and reconnect with the real world.

Thank you for picking up this book. I hope it serves as a helpful guide on your journey to a healthier, more balanced relationship with technology. Enjoy the book, and remember to take the time to detox.

PURPOSE OF THE BOOK

The purpose of "Digital Detox: 10 Easy Tips to Unplug and Recharge" is to provide practical guidance and support for individuals who feel overwhelmed by their dependence on technology. In today's fast-paced digital world, many of us find ourselves inundated with notifications, social media updates, and the constant pressure to be online. This constant connectivity can lead to burnout, stress, and a diminished quality of life.

In my own life, I experienced firsthand the challenges of managing a healthy relationship with technology. The realization that I was no longer in control of my time and attention prompted me to make a change. I took steps to reclaim my life from the digital chaos, and through this process, I discovered effective strategies to unplug and recharge.

This book is a culmination of those strategies. It aims to help you:

- **Recognize and Address Digital Overload:** Understand the impact of excessive technology use on your mental and physical well-being, and identify the signs of digital overload in your own life.

- **Implement Practical Tips:** Follow ten easy and actionable tips to reduce your dependence on technology. These tips are designed to fit seamlessly into your daily routine, making it easier to achieve a balanced digital lifestyle.

- **Reclaim Your Time and Attention:** Learn how to set boundaries with technology, manage notifications, and create tech-free zones to regain control over your time and focus.

- **Improve Mental and Emotional Health:** Discover techniques to reduce stress, enhance mindfulness, and foster deeper connections with the physical world and the people around you.

- **Protect Our Future Generations:** Understand the importance of guiding children and teenagers towards healthier tech habits, ensuring they grow up with a balanced approach to technology.

This book is not just about reducing screen time; it's about reclaiming your life from the grips of digital dependency. It's about finding a healthier, more fulfilling way to interact with the world, both online and offline. By following the tips in this book, you can create a sustainable digital detox lifestyle that enhances your well-being and helps you lead a more intentional and connected life.

TABLE OF CONTENTS

Welcome to "Digital Detox: 10 Easy Tips to Unplug and Recharge_____3

Purpose of the Book_____4

INTRODUCTION _____10

The Need for digital detox _____13

The Digital Age _____14

Dilemma _____14

The Need for a Digital Detox _____17

Benefits of _____23

Unplugging_____23

Chapter 1: Assessing Your Digital Life_____28

Chapter 2: _____32

Establishing Digital Boundaries _____32

Chapter 3: _____37

Decluttering Your Digital Space _____37

Chapter 4: Mindful Tech Usage _____41

Chapter 5: _____44

Reconnecting with the Physical World _____44

Chapter 6: Digital Detox for Better Sleep _____ 48

Chapter 7: Nurturing Mental and Emotional Well-being_____52

Chapter 8: Building Healthy Tech Habits _____ 56

Chapter 9: Staying Accountable and Motivated __ 60

Chapter 10:_____64

Sustaining Your _____64

Digital Detox Lifestyle_____64

Conclusion: _____68

Appendix: Additional Resources for Digital Detox 74

10 Digital Detox _____84

Exercises _____84

In Closing_____89

INTRODUCTION

- The Digital Age Dilemma

- The Need for a Digital Detox

- Benefits of Unplugging

Chapter 1: Assessing Your Digital Life

- Understanding Your Digital Habits

- Recognizing the Signs of Digital Overload

- Setting Personal Goals for Detoxification

Chapter 2: Establishing Digital Boundaries

- Defining Your Digital Boundaries

- Setting Up Tech-Free Zones

- Creating a Digital Schedule

Chapter 3: Decluttering Your Digital Space

- Organizing Your Devices

- Managing Your Digital Files

- Deleting Unnecessary Apps and Accounts

Chapter 4: Mindful Tech Usage

- Practicing Mindfulness in the Digital World

- Reducing Social Media Consumption

- Limiting Screen Time

Chapter 5: Reconnecting with the Physical World

- Rediscovering Face-to-Face Interaction

- Pursuing Offline Hobbies and Activities

- Embracing Nature and Outdoor Adventures

Chapter 6: Digital Detox for Better Sleep

- Understanding the Impact of Screens on Sleep

- Creating a Relaxing Bedtime Routine

- Sleep-Boosting Tips and Tricks

Chapter 7: Nurturing Mental and Emotional Well-being

- Managing Digital Stress

- Finding Balance in a Connected World

- Meditation and Mindfulness Techniques

Chapter 8: Building Healthy Tech Habits

- Setting Digital Detox Challenges

- Cultivating Sustainable Tech Habits

- Fostering Digital Literacy

Chapter 9: Staying Accountable and Motivated

- The Role of Support Systems

- Tracking Your Progress

- Overcoming Digital Detox Challenges

Chapter 10: Sustaining Your Digital Detox Lifestyle

- Integrating Digital Detox into Daily Life

- Celebrating Your Success

- Embracing a Balanced Digital Future

Conclusion

- The Ongoing Journey of Digital Detox

- Final Thoughts and Encouragement

Exercises

- Revitalize and Reconnect: 10 Simple exercises for a Digital Detox

THE NEED FOR DIGITAL DETOX

In today's fast-paced, hyperconnected world, our digital devices have become an integral part of our lives. We rely on smartphones, tablets, and computers for work, communication, entertainment, and information. While these technological advancements have undoubtedly brought numerous benefits, they've also given rise to a modern dilemma: digital overload. Many of us find ourselves constantly glued to screens, overwhelmed by notifications, and struggling to maintain a healthy work-life-tech balance.

The need for a digital detox has never been more pressing. This book, "Digital Detox: 10 Easy Tips to Unplug and Recharge," explores the challenges posed by our ever-connected existence and offers practical guidance on how to regain control over your digital life. Through a series of manageable steps, you'll discover the transformative power of unplugging and recharging, allowing you to lead a more mindful and balanced life.

THE DIGITAL AGE DILEMMA

While technology has revolutionized the way we live, it has also introduced new stressors and distractions. We'll discuss the impact of constant connectivity on our mental and emotional well-being, relationships, and productivity. By understanding the digital age dilemma, you'll gain insight into why a digital detox is essential for your overall health and happiness.

Technology has undeniably transformed our lives in countless positive ways. It has made information more accessible, connected us with people across the globe, and streamlined countless daily tasks. However, this digital revolution has also brought about significant challenges that we must navigate carefully.

The Constant Connectivity

In the digital age, we are always connected. Our smartphones, tablets, and laptops keep us perpetually plugged into a stream of emails, social media updates, news alerts, and messages. While this connectivity offers convenience, it also means we are never truly "off." This constant state of availability can lead to increased stress and anxiety as we feel compelled to respond to every notification immediately. The expectation of instant communication can create a relentless cycle of pressure and distraction.

Mental and Emotional Well-being

The impact of constant connectivity on our mental and emotional well-being is profound. Studies have shown that excessive screen time is associated with higher levels of stress, anxiety, and depression. The barrage of information and stimuli can overwhelm our brains, leading to cognitive overload and difficulty concentrating. Moreover, the addictive nature of social media can foster feelings of inadequacy and low self-esteem as we compare our lives to the curated, often idealized images we see online.

Strained Relationships

Our relationships, both personal and professional, can suffer in the digital age. The intrusion of technology into our personal lives means that we are often distracted during face-to-face interactions, leading to a decline in the quality of our relationships. The constant need to check our devices can prevent us from being fully present with our loved ones, eroding intimacy and connection. In professional settings, the expectation of being always available can blur the lines between work and personal life, contributing to burnout and resentment.

Decreased Productivity

While technology has the potential to enhance productivity, it can also be a significant source of distraction. The constant interruptions from notifications and the temptation to check social media or other non-work-related sites can severely hinder our ability to focus. Multitasking, often seen as a necessary skill in the digital age, has been shown to reduce efficiency and increase errors. The result is a decrease in overall productivity and a sense of frustration and inadequacy.

THE NEED FOR A DIGITAL DETOX

In our hyper-connected world, the concept of a digital detox is not just a trendy buzzword but an urgent necessity for our overall well-being. As technology continues to permeate every aspect of our lives, it is increasingly important to recognize the signs of digital overload and understand the profound impact it can have on our mental, emotional, and physical health. By identifying these symptoms in your own life, you can begin to appreciate the critical need to take a step back from your screens and reevaluate your relationship with technology.

SIGNS OF DIGITAL OVERLOAD

ANXIETY

One of the most common signs of digital overload is increased anxiety. Constant notifications, emails, and social media updates can create a persistent feeling of being on edge. The pressure to respond immediately to messages and the fear of missing out (FOMO) on important information or social events can exacerbate anxiety levels. Additionally, the endless stream of news, often highlighting negative events, can contribute to a heightened sense of worry and unease.

SLEEP DISTURBANCES

Technology use, particularly in the evening, can significantly disrupt sleep patterns. The blue light emitted by screens interferes with the production of melatonin, a hormone that regulates sleep. This can make it difficult to fall asleep and stay asleep, leading to poor sleep quality and fatigue. Moreover, the mental stimulation from engaging with digital content right before bed can keep your mind active, making it harder to unwind and achieve restful sleep.

REDUCED ATTENTION SPAN

The constant barrage of information and stimuli from digital devices can severely impact our ability to focus and maintain attention. Multitasking, frequent interruptions, and the habit of quickly switching between tasks can lead to a fragmented attention span. This not only affects productivity and efficiency but also impairs our ability to engage deeply with any single activity, reducing the overall quality of our work and experiences.

PHYSICAL SYMPTOMS

Digital overload is not limited to mental and emotional symptoms; it can also manifest physically. Prolonged screen time can lead to eye strain, headaches, and physical discomfort, often referred to as "tech neck" or "text neck." Additionally, the sedentary lifestyle associated with excessive technology use can contribute to poor posture, weight gain, and other health issues related to inactivity.

EMOTIONAL DISCONNECT

Despite being constantly connected digitally, many people feel emotionally disconnected from those around them. The superficial nature of online interactions can leave us feeling isolated and lonely. Real-life relationships can suffer as we become more engrossed in our digital lives, leading to weakened bonds with family and friends.

THE CRITICAL NEED FOR A DIGITAL DETOX

Recognizing these signs of digital overload underscores the urgent need for a digital detox. Taking a deliberate break from technology allows you to reset and restore balance in your life. Here are some reasons why a digital detox is crucial:

- **Mental Clarity:** Stepping away from the constant stream of digital stimuli can help clear your mind, reduce stress, and improve your ability to concentrate.

- **Improved Sleep:** Reducing screen time, especially before bed, can enhance the quality of your sleep, leading to better overall health and well-being.

- **Enhanced Relationships:** Disconnecting from digital devices allows you to be more present with loved ones, fostering deeper, more meaningful connections.

- **Physical Health:** Taking breaks from screens encourages more physical activity and reduces the risk of physical discomfort associated with prolonged screen time.

- **Emotional Well-being:** A digital detox can help alleviate feelings of anxiety and depression, leading to a more balanced and positive outlook on life.

- **Productivity and Creativity:** By minimizing distractions, you can boost your productivity and creativity, allowing you to engage more deeply with your work and hobbies.

TAKING THE FIRST STEP

The journey to a healthier relationship with technology begins with awareness. By recognizing the signs of digital overload in your own life, you can take the first step towards a digital detox. This book will provide you with practical tips and strategies to unplug and recharge, helping you reclaim your time, attention, and overall well-being.

Remember, a digital detox is not about completely eliminating technology from your life but about finding a healthier balance that enhances your quality of life. Embrace this opportunity to take control of your digital habits and create a more mindful, intentional approach to technology use. Your journey towards a more balanced and fulfilling life starts here.

BENEFITS OF UNPLUGGING

Embracing a digital detox lifestyle offers a multitude of benefits that can significantly enhance your overall well-being. In this section, we will highlight the positive outcomes you can expect from making this change. By understanding these benefits, you'll be motivated to incorporate digital detox strategies into your daily life and experience the transformative effects of unplugging.

IMPROVED MENTAL HEALTH

One of the most significant benefits of a digital detox is the improvement in mental health. Constant exposure to digital stimuli can lead to anxiety, stress, and even depression. By taking regular breaks from technology, you allow your mind to rest and recover. This can lead to a reduction in anxiety levels, a calmer state of mind, and an overall sense of well-being. Additionally, unplugging gives you the opportunity to engage in mindfulness practices, such as meditation and deep breathing, which further contribute to mental clarity and emotional stability.

INCREASED PRODUCTIVITY

Disconnecting from digital distractions can lead to a substantial increase in productivity. Without the constant interruptions from notifications and the temptation to check social media, you can focus more deeply on tasks at hand. This enhanced focus allows you to work more efficiently and complete tasks with greater accuracy. A digital detox helps you prioritize your responsibilities and manage your time more effectively, leading to higher productivity and a greater sense of accomplishment.

STRONGER PERSONAL RELATIONSHIPS

Technology, while connecting us globally, can often disconnect us from the people physically present in our lives. By unplugging, you create more opportunities for face-to-face interactions and meaningful conversations with loved ones. This fosters deeper connections and strengthens personal relationships. When you are fully present in your interactions, you show others that you value their company, which can lead to more fulfilling and rewarding relationships.

ENHANCED CREATIVITY

Constant exposure to digital content can overwhelm our creative faculties, making it difficult to generate original ideas. A digital detox provides the mental space needed for creativity to flourish. By stepping away from screens and engaging in offline activities, such as reading, writing, painting, or exploring nature, you can stimulate your imagination and think more creatively. This break from digital overload can lead to a renewed sense of inspiration and innovative thinking.

BETTER PHYSICAL HEALTH

Reducing screen time has notable benefits for your physical health. Prolonged use of digital devices can lead to eye strain, headaches, and poor posture. By taking regular breaks from screens, you give your eyes and body a much-needed rest. Additionally, unplugging encourages more physical activity, whether it's going for a walk, practicing yoga, or engaging in outdoor sports. These activities not only improve your physical health but also contribute to a better overall quality of life.

GREATER EMOTIONAL RESILIENCE

A digital detox can help build emotional resilience by reducing the negative impact of social media comparisons and the constant influx of information. When you take a step back from the digital world, you can focus more on your own life and goals, rather than being influenced by the curated lives of others. This shift in focus allows you to develop a stronger sense of self-worth and confidence, making you more resilient to external pressures and stresses.

INCREASED PRESENCE AND MINDFULNESS

Unplugging from digital devices promotes a greater sense of presence and mindfulness in everyday life. Without the distractions of notifications and digital content, you can fully engage in the present moment. This heightened awareness allows you to appreciate the simple joys of life, such as a beautiful sunset, a conversation with a friend, or the taste of a delicious meal. Practicing mindfulness through a digital detox can lead to a more fulfilling and enriched life experience.

THE INVITATION TO CHANGE

This book is your guide to experiencing these profound benefits. By the end of "Digital Detox: 10 Easy Tips to Unplug and Recharge," you will have the tools and strategies necessary to take control of your digital habits and create a more balanced and fulfilling life. The journey towards a digital detox is not just about reducing screen time; it's about enhancing your mental, emotional, and physical well-being, strengthening your relationships, and unleashing your creativity.

This introduction sets the stage for the rest of the book, providing you with a compelling rationale for why you should consider a digital detox and what you can hope to achieve through the process. It's an invitation to explore the book's practical tips and insights, helping you lead a more balanced and fulfilling life in the digital age. Embrace the journey, and discover the transformative power of unplugging and recharging.

CHAPTER 1: ASSESSING YOUR DIGITAL LIFE

In the digital age, our lives have become intricately intertwined with technology. Before you embark on your digital detox journey, it's crucial to take a step back and assess your current digital landscape. Chapter 1 serves as a foundational chapter, helping you gain clarity about your digital habits and their impact on your life.

UNDERSTANDING YOUR DIGITAL HABITS

Understanding your digital habits is the first step towards an effective digital detox. In this section, you'll embark on a self-discovery journey to identify how and why you use digital devices. It's a chance to examine your daily routines, such as:

1. **Screen Time Analysis:** Track how much time you spend on different devices and apps each day. This eye-opening exercise often reveals surprising insights about where your attention is focused.

2. **Online Activities:** Take note of your most frequent online activities, whether it's social media scrolling, work-related tasks, or entertainment consumption.

3. **Emotional Triggers:** Recognize the emotional triggers that lead you to use digital devices excessively. Are you using technology to cope with stress, boredom, or loneliness?

4. **Communication Patterns:** Reflect on your communication style and frequency. Are you constantly checking messages and notifications?

By gaining a deep understanding of your digital habits, you'll be better equipped to make informed decisions about which areas of your digital life need adjustment.

RECOGNIZING THE SIGNS OF DIGITAL OVERLOAD

Digital overload is a common consequence of excessive screen time and constant connectivity. In this section, you'll learn to recognize the signs and symptoms of digital overload, which can include:

1. **Increased Stress:** Feeling overwhelmed by a constant influx of information and notifications.

2. **Sleep Disturbances:** Difficulty falling asleep or staying asleep due to late-night screen use.

3. **Reduced Productivity:** Struggling to focus on tasks or experiencing a decrease in productivity.

4. **Impaired Relationships:** Neglecting face-to-face interactions in favor of virtual communication.

5. **Physical Health Issues:** Experiencing physical discomfort like eye strain, headaches, or poor posture from extended screen use.

By identifying these signs in your life, you'll gain a clear picture of the areas that require attention and change.

SETTING PERSONAL GOALS FOR DETOXIFICATION

In the final part of Chapter 1, you'll learn the importance of setting clear and achievable goals for your digital detox. These goals will serve as your roadmap throughout the detox process. They can include:

1. **Screen Time Limits:** Determining specific time limits for daily screen use.

2. **Tech-Free Zones:** Designating areas or times in your home where technology is not allowed.

3. **Reconnecting with Nature:** Committing to spending more time outdoors and away from screens.

4. **Mindful Tech Usage:** Implementing mindfulness techniques to use technology more intentionally.

5. **Improved Sleep:** Establishing a sleep-friendly digital routine.

By setting these goals, you'll have a concrete plan for your digital detox journey. These goals will be revisited and refined as you progress through the chapters of the book, helping you achieve a balanced and healthier relationship with technology.

CHAPTER 2: ESTABLISHING DIGITAL BOUNDARIES

In the digital age, maintaining a healthy balance between your online and offline life often necessitates setting clear and firm digital boundaries. This chapter is dedicated to helping you create those boundaries to regain control over your digital world.

DEFINING YOUR DIGITAL BOUNDARIES

The first step in establishing digital boundaries is defining what these boundaries mean to you personally. In

this section, you'll explore the aspects of your life where digital boundaries are crucial:

1. **Personal Life vs. Digital Life:** Reflect on your priorities and values. Determine how you want to allocate your time and attention between your personal life and your digital life.

2. **Work-Life Balance:** Assess how technology affects your work-life balance. Consider when it's appropriate to disconnect from work-related emails and messages.

3. **Social Media Usage:** Determine how much time and energy you're willing to invest in social media. De-

cide which platforms are essential and which you can reduce or eliminate.

4. **Privacy and Security:** Evaluate your digital boundaries concerning data privacy and online security. Understand how to protect your personal information and maintain a safe online presence.

By defining your digital boundaries, you'll create a framework that aligns with your values and helps you set clear expectations for yourself and those around you.

SETTING UP TECH-FREE ZONES

Tech-free zones are designated areas or times where technology is off-limits. Establishing these zones can help you disconnect from your devices and foster more meaningful, tech-free interactions with the world around you:

1. **Home Zones:** Determine specific areas in your home where technology is not allowed. For example,

the dining table can become a tech-free zone during meals, encouraging face-to-face conversations.

2. **Bedroom Rules:** Create boundaries for tech usage in the bedroom to improve sleep quality. Consider banning screens an hour before bedtime.

3. **Family and Social Gatherings:** Encourage tech-free interactions during family gatherings or social events to enhance personal connections and reduce distractions.

4. **Nature and Outdoor Zones:** Designate specific outdoor times when you'll disconnect from screens to appreciate nature and physical activity fully.

By implementing tech-free zones, you'll reclaim physical spaces for non-digital activities, fostering more mindful and meaningful experiences.

CREATING A DIGITAL SCHEDULE

A digital schedule helps you structure your day to strike a balance between digital engagement and disconnection:

1. **Daily Routines:** Plan your digital activities around specific times of the day. For instance, allocate a set time for checking emails or social media.

2. **Prioritizing Tasks:** Organize your digital tasks based on importance and urgency. This helps you allocate more time to essential activities and minimize distractions.

3. **Scheduled Breaks:** Incorporate regular breaks into your digital schedule to refresh your mind and reduce screen fatigue.

4. **Tech-Free Times:** Designate times during the day when you'll disconnect entirely from screens, allowing your mind to unwind and focus on other activities.

Creating a digital schedule empowers you to be intentional about your tech usage, ensuring that it enhances your life rather than dominates it. It helps you strike a balance between productivity, leisure, and disconnection, ultimately leading to a healthier relationship with technology.

CHAPTER 3: DECLUTTERING YOUR DIGITAL SPACE

As you progress in your digital detox journey, it's essential to declutter your digital space to reduce digital distractions, streamline your workflow, and simplify your online life.

ORGANIZING YOUR DEVICES

Effectively organizing your digital devices is the first step in decluttering your digital space:

1. **Device Inventory:** Begin by taking an inventory of all the digital devices you own, such as smartphones, tablets, laptops, and desktop computers.

2. **Device Cleanup:** Clean and organize your devices physically. Remove dust, debris, and unnecessary cables. Ensure your devices are in good working order.

3. **App Management:** Review the apps on your devices. Uninstall apps that you no longer use or that contribute to excessive screen time. Organize your home screen to prioritize essential apps and reduce visual clutter.

4. **Device Categories:** Consider categorizing your devices based on their purpose. For example, designate one device primarily for work-related tasks and another for personal use.

By organizing your devices, you create a more efficient and purposeful digital environment that supports your detox goals.

MANAGING YOUR DIGITAL FILES

Digital clutter isn't limited to devices; it also includes disorganized digital files:

1. **File Organization:** Start by sorting through your digital files, such as documents, photos, and videos. Create folders and subfolders to categorize and store them logically.

2. **Cloud Storage:** Utilize cloud storage services like Google Drive, Dropbox, or iCloud to back up and organize your files. This helps you access your documents from anywhere while keeping your device storage tidy.

3. **Digital Archive:** Archive or delete old and unnecessary files to free up space. Be selective about what you keep, retaining only what's truly meaningful or useful.

4. **Backup Strategy:** Implement a regular backup strategy to protect your important files from loss. This can include automated backups or periodic manual backups.

By managing your digital files effectively, you reduce clutter, enhance productivity, and ensure that your digital space remains organized and accessible.

DELETING UNNECESSARY APPS AND ACCOUNTS

Over time, you may accumulate a multitude of apps and online accounts, many of which are no longer relevant or necessary:

1. **App Audit:** Conduct a thorough audit of your apps on all devices. Delete apps that serve no purpose or that contribute to digital distractions.

2. **Account Cleanup:** Review your online accounts, including social media, email, and subscription services. Cancel or deactivate accounts that you no longer use or need.

3. **Password Management:** Use a password manager to organize and secure your login credentials. This simplifies your online presence and enhances security.

4. **Email Cleanup:** Declutter your email inbox by unsubscribing from newsletters and promotions that no longer interest you. Create filters to automatically categorize and organize incoming emails.

By deleting unnecessary apps and accounts, you minimize digital noise and reduce the cognitive load associated with managing numerous online profiles. This decluttering process leads to a more streamlined and intentional digital existence, aligning with the goals of your digital detox journey.

CHAPTER 4: MINDFUL TECH USAGE

Mindful tech usage is about consciously engaging with technology in a way that enhances your well-being and minimizes digital distractions. This chapter explores practical strategies for achieving a more mindful relationship with your digital devices.

PRACTICING MINDFULNESS IN THE DIGITAL WORLD

1. **Digital Mindfulness Techniques:** Learn mindfulness techniques that can be applied to your digital life. This includes practices like mindful breathing, where you take a moment to breathe deeply and center yourself before interacting with your devices.

2. **Mindful Notifications:** Customize your device's notification settings to reduce interruptions. Disable

non-essential notifications and prioritize those that truly matter, allowing you to stay focused when needed.

3. **Single-Tasking:** Embrace the art of single-tasking instead of multitasking. Focus on one digital task at a time, whether it's responding to emails, working on a project, or engaging in online conversations.

4. **Scheduled Tech Breaks:** Incorporate scheduled tech breaks into your day to step away from screens. Use these breaks for short walks, stretching exercises, or simply to disconnect and clear your mind.

Reducing Social Media Consumption

1. **Audit Your Social Media Use:** Analyze your social media habits. Identify which platforms you spend the most time on and assess the impact they have on your well-being.

2. **Unfollow and Unsubscribe:** Unfollow or mute accounts that don't bring value to your life. Unsubscribe from groups, pages, or newsletters that no longer interest you.

3. **Set Usage Limits:** Utilize built-in app features or third-party apps to set daily or weekly usage limits for social media platforms. This helps prevent mindless scrolling.

4. **Designate Social Media Time:** Allocate specific time slots in your daily schedule for social media use. Stick to these designated times to avoid compulsive checking.

LIMITING SCREEN TIME

1. **Screen Time Tracking:** Use screen time tracking features on your devices to monitor your daily screen usage. This provides valuable insights into your habits.

2. **Digital Sabbaticals:** Consider taking periodic digital sabbaticals, which involve completely disconnecting from screens for a set period, such as a weekend or a week.

3. **Nighttime Wind-Down:** Establish a nighttime wind-down routine that includes reducing screen time at least an hour before bedtime. Engaging in calming

activities like reading or meditation can improve sleep quality.

4. **Family Screen Time Rules:** If you have a family, set screen time rules that everyone follows. This can include designated tech-free hours or activities that promote in-person interactions.

By practicing mindfulness, reducing social media consumption, and limiting screen time, you'll regain control over your digital life. These strategies empower you to use technology as a tool for enhancing your life rather than allowing it to dominate your time and attention. A mindful approach to tech usage fosters greater balance, focus, and well-being in the digital age.

CHAPTER 5: RECONNECTING WITH THE PHYSICAL WORLD

In the digital age, it's crucial to find ways to reconnect with the physical world and foster genuine experiences beyond screens. This chapter explores strategies to do just that.

REDISCOVERING FACE-TO-FACE INTERACTION

1. **Prioritize In-Person Conversations:** Make an effort to prioritize face-to-face conversations with friends, family, and colleagues. Engage in meaningful discussions, share experiences, and strengthen your personal connections.

2. **Tech-Free Zones for Gatherings:** Designate tech-free zones during social gatherings or meals to encourage genuine interactions. This can help create a space where everyone is fully present.

3. **Active Listening:** Practice active listening during conversations. Put away your phone and give your full attention to the person you're speaking with, fostering deeper and more empathetic communication.

4. **Plan Social Activities:** Organize social activities that involve physical presence, such as game nights, hiking trips, or attending local events together.

PURSUING OFFLINE HOBBIES AND ACTIVITIES

1. **Identify Offline Hobbies:** Discover or reignite hobbies that don't involve screens. This could include reading physical books, cooking, painting, playing musical instruments, or crafting.

2. **Join Local Clubs or Groups:** Explore local clubs or interest groups related to your offline hobbies. Engaging with like-minded individuals can provide a sense of community and support.

3. **Set Hobby Goals:** Set achievable goals for your offline hobbies, such as finishing a novel, mastering a new recipe, or completing a woodworking project. This gives you a sense of accomplishment and purpose.

4. Offline Learning: Consider taking up a new skill or hobby through offline classes or workshops in your community. Learning in a hands-on, face-to-face setting can be highly rewarding.

EMBRACING NATURE AND OUTDOOR ADVENTURES

1. **Nature Walks:** Spend time outdoors, whether it's taking leisurely walks in the park, hiking in the wilderness, or exploring nearby trails. Nature offers a peaceful escape from the digital world.

2. **Outdoor Activities:** Engage in outdoor activities like camping, fishing, birdwatching, or gardening. These activities not only connect you with nature but also provide a sense of accomplishment.

3. **Digital Detox Retreats:** Consider attending digital detox retreats or wellness camps that offer structured programs for disconnecting from screens and embracing nature.

4. **Mindful Nature Practices:** Practice mindfulness in nature by observing the sights, sounds, and sensations around you. This can help reduce stress and improve your overall well-being.

Reconnecting with the physical world is essential for maintaining a balanced and fulfilling life. By prioritizing face-to-face interactions, pursuing offline hobbies, and embracing the beauty of nature, you can counter the often isolating and sedentary nature of digital technology. These activities not only promote well-being but also enhance your overall quality of life, allowing you to experience the world in all its richness and diversity.

CHAPTER 6: DIGITAL DETOX FOR BETTER SLEEP

Quality sleep is essential for physical and mental well-being, yet our digital devices can often disrupt our sleep patterns. This chapter focuses on the relationship between digital detox and improving your sleep.

Understanding the Impact of Screens on Sleep

1. **The Role of Blue Light:** Screens emit blue light, which can interfere with your body's production of melatonin, a hormone that regulates sleep. Exposure to screens, especially before bedtime, can delay the onset of sleep.

2. **Increased Mental Stimulation:** Engaging with screens, whether through work, social media, or entertainment, can mentally stimulate you, making it difficult to relax and fall asleep.

3. **Sleep Disruption:** Notifications and the urge to check emails or social media during the night can lead to sleep disruptions, causing you to wake up multiple times.

4. **Disrupted Circadian Rhythm:** Prolonged screen use, particularly late at night, can disrupt your circadian rhythm, making it challenging to maintain a consistent sleep schedule.

Understanding how screens affect your sleep is the first step in addressing sleep-related issues resulting from digital device usage.

CREATING A RELAXING BEDTIME ROUTINE

1. **Set a Screen Curfew:** Establish a screen curfew at least an hour before bedtime. This gives your brain time to unwind and prepare for sleep.

2. **Blue Light Filters:** Use blue light filters on your devices or invest in blue light-blocking glasses to reduce the impact of screens on your melatonin production.

3. **Wind-Down Activities:** Incorporate relaxing activities into your bedtime routine. This can include reading a physical book, taking a warm bath, or practicing gentle yoga or meditation.

4. **Create a Sleep-Inducing Environment:** Ensure your bedroom is conducive to sleep. Keep it cool, dark, and quiet. Invest in a comfortable mattress and pillows to maximize comfort.

SLEEP-BOOSTING TIPS AND TRICKS

1. **Establish a Consistent** Sleep Schedule: Go to bed and wake up at the same times each day, even on weekends. This helps regulate your circadian rhythm.

2. **Limit Caffeine and Alcohol:** Avoid consuming caffeine and alcohol close to bedtime, as they can interfere with sleep quality.

3. **Exercise Regularly:** Engage in regular physical activity, but avoid strenuous exercise close to bedtime. Exercise can improve sleep quality and help you fall asleep faster.

4. **Mindfulness and Relaxation Techniques:** Practice relaxation techniques like deep breathing, progressive muscle relaxation, or mindfulness meditation to calm your mind and reduce anxiety that may impact sleep.

5. **Limit Screen Access During the Night:** Keep your devices out of reach or in another room during the night to prevent the temptation to check them if you wake up.

6. **Seek Professional Help:** If you continue to experience sleep problems despite implementing these

strategies, consider consulting a healthcare professional or sleep specialist for guidance and support.

By understanding the impact of screens on your sleep, creating a relaxing bedtime routine, and implementing sleep-boosting tips and tricks, you can significantly improve your sleep quality and overall well-being. A digital detox before bedtime can lead to more restful and rejuvenating sleep, allowing you to wake up feeling refreshed and ready to tackle the day ahead.

CHAPTER 7: NURTURING MENTAL AND EMOTIONAL WELL-BEING

In today's fast-paced digital world, nurturing your mental and emotional well-being is crucial for a balanced and fulfilling life. This chapter focuses on strategies for managing digital stress, finding balance in a hyperconnected world, and incorporating meditation and mindfulness techniques into your daily routine.

MANAGING DIGITAL STRESS

1. **Identifying Stressors:** Recognize the specific digital stressors in your life. These may include information overload, constant notifications, work-related pressures, or social media comparison.

2. **Establish Boundaries:** Set clear boundaries between work and personal life, and create designated tech-free times and spaces. This helps reduce the constant pressure to be connected.

3. **Practice Digital Detox Days:** Dedicate entire days or weekends to digital detox. Disconnect from screens entirely and engage in offline activities that relax and rejuvenate you.

4. **Prioritize Self-Care:** Make self-care a priority by engaging in activities that reduce stress, such as exercise, journaling, spending time in nature, or pursuing hobbies.

5. **Seek Support:** Share your digital stress concerns with friends, family, or a therapist. Talking about your experiences can provide emotional support and new perspectives.

FINDING BALANCE IN A CONNECTED WORLD

1. **Set Realistic Expectations:** Understand that you don't have to be constantly available or online. Set realistic expectations for yourself and communicate your boundaries to others.

2. **Offline Quality Time:** Allocate dedicated quality time with loved ones without digital distractions. This strengthens your personal relationships and fosters a sense of connection.

3. **Digital Work-Life Balance:** Strive to maintain a healthy work-life balance by setting clear working hours and disconnecting from work-related communications during personal time.

4. **Embrace Tech Sabbaticals:** Periodically take tech sabbaticals to completely disconnect from screens. Use this time to recharge, reflect, and engage in offline activities.

5. **Practice Gratitude:** Cultivate gratitude by focusing on the positive aspects of technology, such as staying connected with loved ones, accessing valuable information, or enjoying entertainment.

MEDITATION AND MINDFULNESS TECHNIQUES

1. **Mindful Tech Use:** Apply mindfulness to your tech usage by being fully present when engaging with screens. Notice how technology affects your thoughts, emotions, and physical sensations.

2. **Daily Meditation:** Establish a daily meditation practice, even if it's just a few minutes each day. Meditation can help reduce stress, improve focus, and enhance overall well-being.

3. **Breathing Exercises:** Incorporate simple breathing exercises throughout your day to center yourself and reduce digital stress. Deep, mindful breaths can have an immediate calming effect.

4. **Mindful Walking:** Practice mindful walking, whether it's in nature or simply around your neighborhood. Pay attention to each step, your surroundings, and the sensation of movement.

5. **Digital Detox Retreats:** Consider attending digital detox retreats or mindfulness workshops that combine technology breaks with guided mindfulness practices.

Nurturing your mental and emotional well-being in the digital age requires a deliberate and proactive approach. By managing digital stress, finding balance in your connected world, and incorporating meditation and mindfulness techniques into your daily life, you can foster a sense of inner peace, resilience, and clarity in the face of digital distractions and challenges.

CHAPTER 8: BUILDING HEALTHY TECH HABITS

Building healthy tech habits is essential for maintaining a balanced and fulfilling relationship with technology. This chapter explores strategies for setting digital detox challenges, cultivating sustainable tech habits, and fostering digital literacy.

SETTING DIGITAL DETOX CHALLENGES

1. **Define Your Challenge:** Start by defining the parameters of your digital detox challenge. This could include a specific duration (e.g., a weekend, a week, or a month) or a focus area (e.g., social media detox, email reduction, or screen time limits).

2. **Communicate Your Goals:** Inform friends, family, or colleagues about your digital detox challenge. Sharing your goals with others can help you stay accountable and receive support.

3. **Track Progress:** Keep a journal or use a digital app to track your progress during the challenge. Record your experiences, emotions, and any insights gained during the detox.

4. **Celebrate Milestones:** Celebrate your achievements along the way. Acknowledge and reward your-

self for reaching milestones, such as successfully completing a week without social media or significantly reducing screen time.

5. **Reflect and Adjust:** After completing a digital detox challenge, reflect on what you've learned and how it has impacted your life. Use these insights to make adjustments to your ongoing tech habits.

CULTIVATING SUSTAINABLE TECH HABITS

1. **Start Small:** When forming new tech habits, start with manageable changes. Gradually increase the complexity of your habits as you build consistency.

2. **Define Priorities:** Identify your digital priorities. Determine which apps, platforms, or online activities align with your values and goals, and prioritize them over less meaningful ones.

3. **Daily Rituals:** Incorporate daily rituals into your tech habits, such as digital check-ins or screen-free moments for reflection and mindfulness.

4. **Digital Boundaries:** Continue to reinforce and refine your digital boundaries. Regularly assess whether your current tech habits align with your intentions and make adjustments as needed.

5. **Social Support:** Share your tech habit goals with friends or family and invite them to join you. Cultivating tech habits together can create a supportive environment for change.

FOSTERING DIGITAL LITERACY

1. **Stay Informed:** Keep yourself informed about the latest digital trends, privacy concerns, and online safety practices. Understanding the digital landscape empowers you to make informed choices.

2. **Online Resources:** Utilize online resources and courses to enhance your digital literacy. There are numerous free and paid courses available on topics like cybersecurity, digital privacy, and responsible tech use.

3. **Teach Others:** Share your knowledge with friends, family, or colleagues, especially those who may be less

digitally literate. Helping others navigate the digital world can reinforce your own understanding.

4. **Critical Thinking:** Develop critical thinking skills when consuming digital content. Question the accuracy and credibility of information and avoid spreading misinformation.

5. **Privacy Awareness:** Prioritize your online privacy by understanding how data is collected and shared. Take steps to protect your personal information online.

By setting digital detox challenges, cultivating sustainable tech habits, and fostering digital literacy, you not only gain control over your digital life but also become a more responsible and empowered digital citizen. These habits contribute to a healthier and more mindful relationship with technology, allowing you to harness its benefits while minimizing its drawbacks.

CHAPTER 9: STAYING ACCOUNTABLE AND MOTIVATED

Maintaining a digital detox and healthy tech habits requires ongoing commitment and motivation. This chapter focuses on the role of support systems, tracking your progress, and overcoming digital detox challenges to stay on the path to a balanced digital life.

THE ROLE OF SUPPORT SYSTEMS

1. **Identify Your Support Network:** Recognize the people in your life who can support your digital detox journey. This might include friends, family, colleagues, or support groups.

2. **Share Your Goals:** Communicate your digital detox goals with your support network. Let them know why these goals are important to you and how they can assist you in achieving them.

3. **Accountability Partners:** Consider partnering with an accountability buddy who shares similar tech goals. You can check in with each other regularly, share progress, and provide encouragement.

4. **Professional Support:** If you're facing significant digital addiction or tech-related mental health issues,

don't hesitate to seek professional help. Therapists and counselors can provide specialized guidance.

5. **Join Online Communities:** Engage in online communities or forums dedicated to digital detox and healthy tech habits. These platforms offer a sense of belonging and a space to share experiences and strategies.

TRACKING YOUR PROGRESS

1. **Use Digital Tools:** Leverage digital tools and apps to track your progress. There are apps designed to monitor screen time, track digital habits, and even enforce self-imposed limits.

2. **Journaling:** Maintain a digital detox journal where you record your experiences, challenges, and successes. Regular journaling can help you stay mindful of your journey.

3. **Goal Setting:** Continually set and review your tech-related goals. This provides a sense of purpose and direction, helping you stay motivated.

4. **Visualize Your Progress:** Create visual representations of your progress, such as charts or graphs, to visually see how far you've come. Celebrate milestones along the way.

5. **Feedback Loops:** Seek feedback from your support network or accountability partner. Constructive feedback can offer valuable insights and motivation.

OVERCOMING DIGITAL DETOX CHALLENGES

1. **Anticipate Triggers:** Identify common triggers that lead to excessive tech use or digital distractions. Knowing your triggers allows you to proactively address them.

2. **Problem-Solve:** Develop strategies for handling specific challenges. For example, if you often check your phone in bed, consider leaving it outside the bedroom.

3. **Self-Compassion:** Be kind to yourself if you slip up or face setbacks. Understand that change is a process,

and occasional lapses are normal. Use setbacks as opportunities for learning and growth.

4. **Mindfulness Practices:** Continue to practice mindfulness and meditation techniques to stay present and reduce impulsive tech use.

5. **Reevaluate and Adjust:** Regularly review and adjust your digital detox plan as needed. Life circumstances and priorities may change, requiring modifications to your approach.

By leveraging support systems, tracking your progress, and developing strategies to overcome digital detox challenges, you can maintain your commitment to a balanced digital life. Staying accountable and motivated is an ongoing process that involves adapting to new circumstances and continuously striving for a healthier relationship with technology.

CHAPTER 10: SUSTAINING YOUR DIGITAL DETOX LIFESTYLE

Sustaining a digital detox lifestyle involves seamlessly integrating your newfound habits into your daily life, celebrating your successes, and adopting a balanced approach to technology for the future.

Integrating Digital Detox into Daily Life

1. **Establish Routines:** Incorporate your digital detox habits into daily routines. For example, if you've adopted a morning meditation practice, make it a non-negotiable part of your morning ritual.

2. **Set Tech Boundaries:** Maintain the boundaries you've established during your digital detox. Continuously prioritize tech-free times, tech-free zones, and mindful tech usage.

3. **Regular Reflection:** Dedicate time for regular reflection on your digital detox journey. Consider how your life has improved since you began, and remind yourself of the reasons behind your tech habits.

4. **Mindful Decision-Making:** Approach technology with mindfulness and intentionality. Ask yourself whether engaging with a particular app or platform aligns with your values and goals.

5. **Stay Informed:** Keep yourself updated on the latest trends in tech and digital well-being. This knowledge can help you make informed decisions about your tech usage.

CELEBRATING YOUR SUCCESS

1. **Reflect on Achievements:** Take time to reflect on the positive changes you've experienced since embarking on your digital detox journey. Celebrate the milestones you've reached.

2. **Reward Yourself:** Acknowledge and reward yourself for your efforts and achievements. Treat yourself to something special as a token of appreciation for your commitment.

3. **Share Your Success:** Share your digital detox success story with others. Your journey can inspire and motivate those around you to take their own steps toward healthier tech habits.

4. **Gratitude Practice:** Cultivate a gratitude practice by focusing on the ways in which your life has im-

proved through digital detox. Express gratitude for the increased mindfulness and presence in your life.

EMBRACING A BALANCED DIGITAL FUTURE

1. **Continual Growth:** Understand that your digital detox journey is not finite. It's a lifelong process of growth and adaptation. Continue to evolve your tech habits as your life circumstances change.

2. **Flexibility and Adaptation:** Be flexible and open to adjustments. Embrace technology when it enhances your life, and recognize when it's time to take a step back.

3. **Resilience:** Develop resilience in the face of digital temptations and challenges. Practice mindfulness and self-compassion to navigate the digital landscape with confidence.

4. **Modeling Behavior:** Set an example for others by demonstrating the benefits of a balanced tech ap-

proach. Inspire those around you to prioritize their well-being in a digital age.

5. **Stay Aligned with Values:** Regularly assess whether your tech habits align with your evolving values and goals. Make conscious choices that reflect your authentic self.

Sustaining your digital detox lifestyle is a lifelong commitment to well-being and balance. By seamlessly integrating your tech habits into daily life, celebrating your successes, and embracing a balanced digital future, you can enjoy the benefits of technology while preserving the essential aspects of human connection, presence, and mindfulness that contribute to a fulfilling life.

CONCLUSION:

Congratulations on completing your journey of digital detox and taking proactive steps towards a healthier relationship with technology. As you conclude this transformative experience, it's important to reflect on the ongoing nature of your digital detox journey, share final thoughts, and offer encouragement for the road ahead.

THE ONGOING JOURNEY OF DIGITAL DETOX:

Your digital detox journey doesn't end with this book; rather, it's a lifelong commitment to mindful tech usage and digital well-being. Remember that the digital landscape is ever-evolving, and your tech habits must adapt accordingly. The skills you've acquired during your detox–such as setting boundaries, practicing mindfulness, and seeking balance–will continue to serve you well.

Stay open to learning and growing in your digital life. Continue to evaluate and adjust your tech habits as your goals, priorities, and circumstances change. Embrace the flexibility to integrate technology in ways that enrich your life and protect your well-being.

FINAL THOUGHTS AND ENCOURAGEMENT:

As you wrap up your digital detox journey, here are some final thoughts and words of encouragement:

1. **Celebrate Your Achievements:** Take pride in the progress you've made. Celebrate the positive changes you've experienced, whether it's improved focus, stronger relationships, or enhanced overall well-being.

2. **Mindful Tech Usage:** Approach technology with mindfulness and intentionality. Remember that you have the power to choose how you engage with digital devices and platforms. Make choices that align with your values.

3. **Share Your Wisdom:** Share your digital detox journey and knowledge with others. Your experiences and insights can inspire and support those around you who may also be seeking a healthier tech-life balance.

4. **Self-Compassion:** Be kind to yourself as you navigate the digital world. Tech challenges and setbacks are part of the journey. Use them as opportunities for growth and learning rather than sources of guilt or frustration.

5. **Stay Connected:** Maintain a strong connection with the physical world and the people in it. Prioritize face-to-face interactions, offline hobbies, and nature experiences to keep you grounded and connected.

6. **Embrace Technology's Benefits:** Technology has the potential to enhance our lives in countless ways. Continue to leverage it for positive purposes, such as education, communication, and personal growth.

7. **Stay Informed:** Stay informed about digital trends, privacy concerns, and security best practices. Knowledge is a powerful tool for navigating the digital landscape responsibly.

In closing, your digital detox journey is a testament to your commitment to a more intentional and fulfilling life. Remember that this is a journey, not a destination, and it's perfectly normal to experience challenges along the way. With mindfulness, resilience, and a dedication to your well-being, you can continue to thrive in the digital age while staying true to your values and goals. Wishing you a future filled with balance, connection, and digital well-being.

REVITALIZE AND RECONNECT: 10 SIMPLE EXERCISES FOR A DIGITAL DETOX

1. **Mindful Breathing**: Take a few minutes each day to practice deep and mindful breathing. Focus on your breath, inhaling and exhaling slowly. This simple exercise can help reduce stress and increase clarity.

2. **Nature Walks:** Spend time in nature by taking leisurely walks in a park, forest, or by the beach. Immerse yourself in the sights, sounds, and sensations of the natural world.

3. **Digital Detox Day:** Dedicate an entire day to a digital detox. Put away your phone, turn off your computer, and disconnect from the digital world. Use this time for reflection, reading, or outdoor activities.

4. **Journaling:** Keep a journal to record your thoughts, feelings, and experiences. Writing can be a therapeutic way to process emotions and gain insights into your life.

5. **Unplugged Reading:** Choose a physical book or magazine and read without any digital distractions. Create a cozy reading nook and savor the joy of getting lost in a good book.

6. **Yoga and Stretching:** Practice yoga or gentle stretching exercises to release tension in your body. Yoga can also promote mental clarity and relaxation.

7. **Mindful Eating:** Pay close attention to your meals by eating mindfully. Slow down, savor each bite, and fully appreciate the flavors and textures of your food.

8. **Tech-Free Socializing:** Spend quality time with friends or family without the distraction of digital devices. Engage in meaningful face-to-face conversations and activities.

9. **Creative Hobbies:** Explore creative hobbies like painting, drawing, playing a musical instrument, or crafting. These activities allow you to express yourself and tap into your creativity.

10. **Digital Sunset:** Establish a "digital sunset" by turning off screens at least an hour before bedtime. Use

this time for relaxation, meditation, or connecting with loved ones.

Incorporating these exercises into your routine can help you recharge, find balance, and cultivate a healthier relationship with technology. Remember that the key is to be consistent and prioritize self-care in the digital age.

APPENDIX: ADDITIONAL RESOURCES FOR DIGITAL DETOX

Embarking on a digital detox journey can be challenging, but there are numerous resources available to support you. This appendix provides a comprehensive list of books, apps, tools, and other resources that can help you unplug and recharge effectively. Use these resources to deepen your understanding, find inspiration, and maintain your digital detox lifestyle.

Resource List for Further Reading

1. **Books:** - Digital Minimalism: Choosing a Focused Life in a Noisy World by Cal Newport

   - **How to Break Up with Your Phone:** The 30-Day Plan to Take Back Your Life* by Catherine Price

   - **The Shallows:** What the Internet Is Doing to Our Brains by Nicholas Carr

   - **Indistractable:** How to Control Your Attention and Choose Your Life by Nir Eyal

   - Reclaiming Conversation: The Power of Talk in a Digital Age by Sherry Turkle

2. **Articles and Reports:**

   - Your Brain on Screens by National Geographic

   - How Smartphones Hijack Our Minds by The Wall Street Journal

   - The Power of a Digital Detox by Psychology Today

   - The Impact of Screen Time on Mental Health by Harvard Health Publishing

DIGITAL DETOX TOOLKIT (APPS, TOOLS, AND RESOURCES)

1. Apps to Help You Unplug:

   - **Forest:** An app that helps you stay focused by planting virtual trees that grow while you stay off your phone.

   - **Moment:** Tracks your phone usage and helps you set limits to reduce screen time.

   - **Freedom:** Blocks distracting websites and apps to help you focus.

   - **Space:** Guides you to phone-life balance by helping you set goals and track progress.

   - **Headspace:** Offers meditation and mindfulness exercises to help reduce stress and increase focus.

2. Tools for Better Digital Habits:

- **Screen Time (iOS) and Digital Wellbeing (Android):** Built-in tools on your smartphone that track usage and allow you to set limits.

- **Pomodoro Timers:** Use a Pomodoro timer to break work into intervals with short breaks, improving focus and reducing screen time.

- **Blue Light Blocking Glasses:** Reduce eye strain from screens with glasses that block blue light.

- **Physical Alarm Clock:** Use a traditional alarm clock to keep your phone out of the bedroom and improve sleep quality.

3. **Online Communities and Support Groups:**

- **Digital Detox Movement:** Join online forums and social media groups dedicated to digital detox practices.

- **Minimalism Community:** Engage with communities focused on minimalism, which often includes digital decluttering.

- **Mindfulness and Meditation Groups:** Participate in groups that encourage mindfulness practices, helping you stay present and reduce screen time.

PERSONAL DIGITAL DETOX JOURNAL

Keeping a journal can be a powerful tool in your digital detox journey. Use the following prompts and templates to reflect on your progress, set goals, and stay motivated.

1. **Daily Reflection Prompts:**

   - How much time did I spend on screens today?

   - What activities did I engage in offline today?

   - How did I feel after reducing my screen time?

   - What challenges did I face in unplugging today?

   - What strategies worked well for me today?

2. **Weekly Review:**

   - Total screen time for the week.

- Successes and achievements in reducing screen time.

- Areas for improvement and strategies to try next week.

- Notable changes in mood, productivity, and relationships.

3. **Goal Setting:**

- Set specific, measurable, attainable, relevant, and time-bound (SMART) goals for your digital detox.

- Examples: "I will reduce my social media use to 30 minutes per day by the end of the month" or "I will have tech-free evenings three times a week."

4. **Mindfulness and Gratitude:**

- Include sections for mindfulness practices and gratitude journaling to help you stay present and appreciate the benefits of unplugging.

- Examples: "Today, I am grateful for the uninterrupted time I spent with my family" or "Practicing yoga without distractions helped me feel more centered."

By utilizing these additional resources, you can enhance your digital detox journey and build a sustainable lifestyle that prioritizes well-being and balance. Remember, the key to a successful digital detox is consistency and mindfulness. Use these tools and strategies to support your efforts and enjoy the many benefits of unplugging and recharging.

WEBSITES AND ONLINE COMMUNITIES

1. **Zoel.com**: I am a musical conscious artist .My music is designed to help listeners tap into their own inner power and connect with their true essence. My music is designed to help us find peace, joy, and happiness, no matter what challenges we may be facing in life

2. **Greater Good Science Center** (greatergood.berkeley.edu): This website offers research-backed articles, tools, and practices for enhancing well-being, gratitude, and happiness.

3. **Themove-ment.com**: Explore mindfulness experiences, to help you stay present and cultivate a positive mindset.

4. **Mindful.org:** Explore mindfulness practices, articles, and resources.

COURSES AND WORKSHOPS

1. **Coursera:** Digital Well-being and Productivity

   - About: This course offers practical strategies to manage your digital life and improve productivity. https://www.coursera.org

2. **Mindful Tech:** Navigating Our Digital World

   - Center for Humane Technology

   - This workshop focuses on mindful tech use and building healthier relationships with digital devices.https://www.humanetech.com

3. **Digital Minimalism Workshop**

- Cal Newport

  - A workshop based on Cal Newport's book *Digital Minimalism*, guiding participants through decluttering their digital lives. https://www.calnewport.com

4. **Mindfulness-Based Stress Reduction (MBSR)**

  - MBSR courses teach mindfulness techniques that can help manage stress and reduce the impact of digital overload. https://www.umassmed.edu/cfm/mindfulness-based-programs/mbsr-courses/

5. **Unplugged: Digital Detox Retreats**

  - Retreats focused on digital detox, offering a break from technology in serene environments. https://www.digitaldetox.org

6. **Digital Well-being and Mindfulness Courses**

  - Udemy

  - A variety of courses that focus on digital well-being, mindfulness, and reducing screen time. https://www.udemy.com

7. **The Science of Well-being**

   - Yale University via Coursera

   - While not solely focused on digital detox, this course helps improve overall well-being, which can complement digital detox efforts. https://www.coursera.org/learn/the-science-of-well-being

8. **Calm Mind:** Digital Detox Program

   - Calm

   - Calm offers a specific program aimed at reducing screen time and improving digital habits through mindfulness and relaxation techniques. https://www.calm.com

9. **Digital Detox Challenge**

   - Simple Habit

   - A guided program designed to help users take a break from their digital devices and foster healthier habits. https://www.simplehabit.com

10. **Offline Balance:** Digital Detox Workshop

- Local wellness centers or community colleges

- Many local institutions offer workshops and seminars focused on achieving a healthy balance with technology.

By participating in these courses and workshops, you can gain valuable insights, practical tools, and supportive communities that will help reinforce your commitment to a digital detox. These resources provide structured guidance and expert advice, making your journey towards a more balanced and fulfilling life even more achievable.

10 DIGITAL DETOX EXERCISES

Use these exercises regularly to cultivate a positive mindset and enhance your well-being. You can adapt and modify them to suit your preferences and needs, ensuring that unplugging and recharging becomes a natural part of your daily life.

1. **Morning Screen-Free Routine**

   - **Exercise**: Start your day without checking your phone or other screens for the first hour. Instead, engage in activities like stretching, meditating, or having a mindful breakfast.

   - **Purpose**: Helps you set a positive tone for the day and reduces immediate stress from notifications.

2. **Tech-Free Meals**

   - **Exercise**: Make all meal times tech-free zones. Focus on enjoying your food and conversing with those around you.

   - **Purpose**: Enhances mindfulness and strengthens personal connections.

3. **Digital Sunset**

   - **Exercise**: Turn off all screens one hour before bedtime. Use this time to relax with a book, journal, or practice meditation.

   - **Purpose**: Improves sleep quality by reducing blue light exposure and promoting relaxation.

4. **Social Media Break**

   - **Exercise**: Take a break from social media for 24 hours once a week. Use the time to engage in offline activities you enjoy.

   - **Purpose**: Reduces anxiety and comparison, helping you to reconnect with your interests and hobbies.

5. **Mindful Walks**

   - **Exercise**: Go for a daily walk without your phone. Pay attention to your surroundings, the sounds, and your breathing.

   - **Purpose**: Promotes mindfulness and physical activity, giving your mind a rest from digital stimuli.

6. **Tech-Free Evenings**

   - **Exercise**: Designate one evening a week as tech-free. Plan activities like board games, cooking, or visiting friends.

   - **Purpose**: Encourages face-to-face interaction and meaningful leisure time.

7. Email Check Schedule

- **Exercise**: Limit checking your email to three specific times a day (morning, midday, and late afternoon). Avoid checking emails outside these times.

- **Purpose**: Reduces constant interruptions and helps you focus on tasks more effectively.

8. Digital Declutter

- **Exercise**: Spend 30 minutes each week organizing your digital files, deleting unnecessary apps, and clearing your inbox.

- **Purpose**: Creates a more organized and less overwhelming digital environment.

9. Mindfulness Meditation

- **Exercise**: Practice a 10-minute mindfulness meditation focusing on your breath, once a day.

- **Purpose**: Helps you become more aware of your digital habits and promotes mental clarity.

10. Tech-Free Commute

- **Exercise**: Use your commute time to listen to music, an audiobook, or simply observe your surroundings instead of using your phone.

  - **Purpose**: Reduces screen time and promotes relaxation before and after work.

MONTHLY REFLECTION

1. What were the most significant changes you noticed after implementing the digital detox exercises?

2. Which exercises were the most challenging to maintain, and why?

3. How has your mental and emotional well-being changed since starting the digital detox?

4. What benefits have you experienced in your personal relationships?

5. What new habits have you formed, and which old habits do you plan to continue reducing?

6. How have your productivity and creativity levels been impacted?

7. What are your goals for the next month regarding digital detox?

By using this guide, you can track your progress, reflect on your experiences, and stay motivated on your journey towards a healthier relationship with technology.

IN CLOSING

As you conclude your journey through "Digital Detox: 10 Easy Tips to Unplug and Recharge," I want to empower you to live a life with balance. By embracing these strategies, you are taking a significant step towards grounding yourself and reconnecting with the world around you.

In this digital age, it's easy to become overwhelmed and disconnected from what truly matters. However, by implementing these tips and exercises, you can reclaim your time, focus, and peace of mind. You will find yourself more present in your daily activities, more connected to the people around you, and more in tune with your own needs and well-being.

Remember, this journey is not about completely eliminating technology from your life. It's about finding a harmonious balance that allows you to enjoy the benefits of technology without being dominated by it. It's about living a life where you are grounded and connected to the earth, to others, and to yourself.

May this book serve as a guide and a companion as you navigate your way towards a more balanced, fulfilling, and mindful life. Embrace the power of unplugging, and discover the richness of a life lived with intention and presence.

Thank you for taking this journey with me. May your life be forever illuminated by the radiant light of positivity. Keep shining." Here's to a future where you control technology, not the other way around. Enjoy your newfound freedom and the countless benefits that come with it. Stay grounded, stay connected, and live a life in balance.

With gratitude and encouragement,

Zoel

"YOU CONTROL YOUR ACTIONS." ZOEL

To learn more about Zoel visit www.zoel.com
Bookings: james@zoel.com

Printed with Love in USA

Printed in Great Britain
by Amazon